Tarquin Number Challenges

GERALD JENKINS

MAGDALEN BEAR

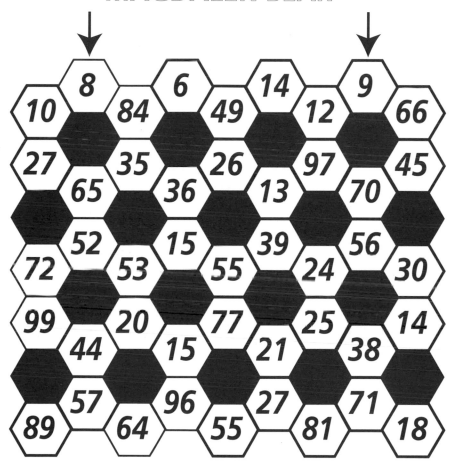

TARQUIN PUBLICATIONS

Challenging Thinking, Puzzling Numbers ...

These demanding and enjoyable puzzles explore some of the hidden properties of numbers and depend on many of the patterns and relationships that exist between them. They make use of the properties of prime numbers, squares, cubes, factors etc. and also investigate the characteristics of magic squares and antimagic squares.

Finding the solutions to these challenges requires a mixture of logical thinking, detective work and often some inspired trial and error. Eliminating what cannot be true is often a good first step along the way to finding out what actually is true. The fundamental step in the breaking of the Enigma Cipher was the realisation that a letter could not translate into itself, a negative piece of information, but of vital importance.

For many of the challenges there are charts, grids and boxes to fill in, making it easier to focus on the steps towards the solution.

To help with some of the puzzles, there are useful lists of primes, squares, factors, factorials etc. on pages 48 and 49.

The authors would like to thank Jon Millington for all his help and support during the preparation of this book.

© 2008 Jenkins & Bear
I.S.B.N: 1 899618 49 X
Design: Magdalen Bear
Printing: Progress Press, Co Ltd
          Malta

Tarquin Publications
99 Hatfield Road
St Albans, Herts
AL1 4JL
United Kingdom
www.tarquinbooks.com

Number Challenge 1

Perfect Cubes

There are twelve perfect cubes with four digits.

1000	1331	1728	2197	2744	3375
4096	4913	5832	6859	8000	9261

Fill in the grid below with the perfect cubes arranged in crossword fashion.

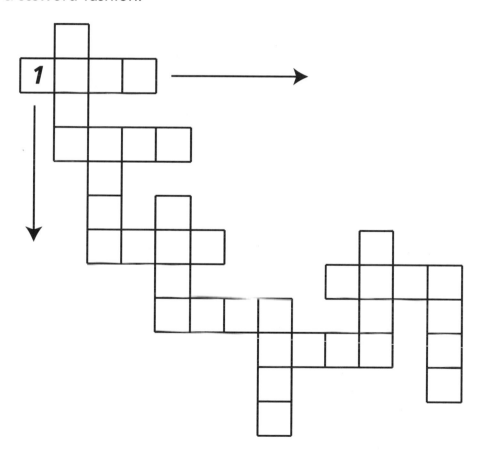

Vertical Pattern Spotting

There is the same hidden relationship between the three numbers in each of the three columns of these diagrams.

In each case discover what it is from the first two and then use it to fill in the blank box.

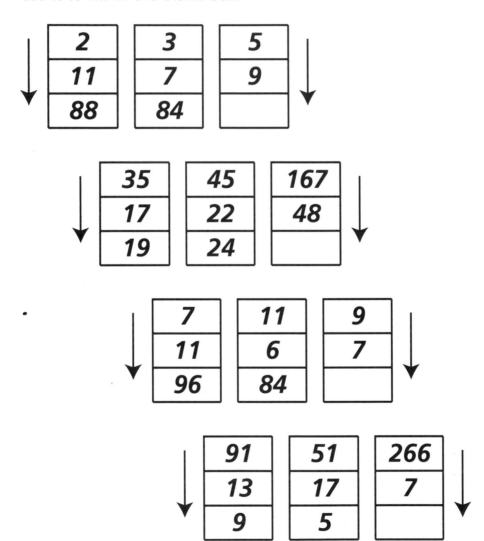

Magic Multiplication Squares

In this multiplication magic square, the numbers in each of the rows, columns and diagonals multiply together to give the same result, 216.

Complete the remaining seven empty squares without repeating any numbers.

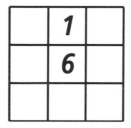

Similarly complete these two magic multiplication squares using each number once only in each square.

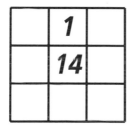

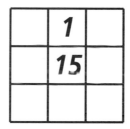

Number Challenge 4

Sum and Difference Cascade

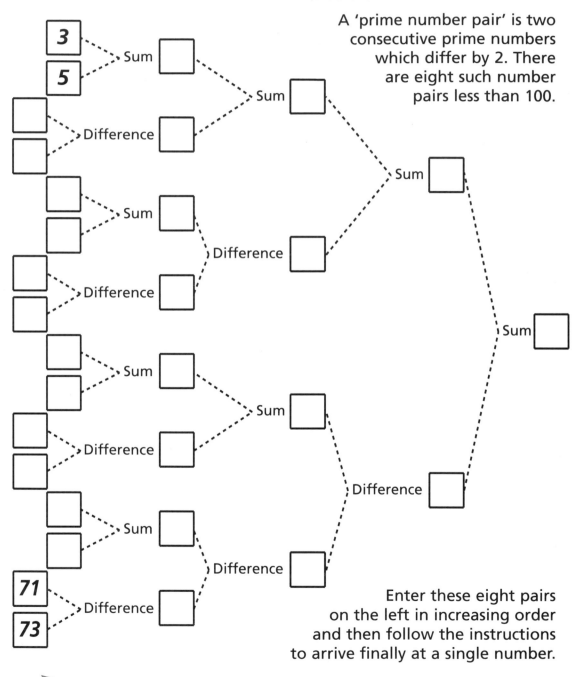

A 'prime number pair' is two consecutive prime numbers which differ by 2. There are eight such number pairs less than 100.

3

5

Sum

Difference

Sum

Difference

Sum

Sum

Difference

Difference

Sum

Sum

Difference

Sum

Difference

Sum

Difference

Sum

71

73

Difference

Enter these eight pairs on the left in increasing order and then follow the instructions to arrive finally at a single number.

6

Number Challenge 5

Finding a Route

The puzzle here is to find a route through each of these grids from top left to bottom right.

Whenever there is a shift to the right there is a multiplication. Whenever there is a shift downwards there is an addition or subtraction.

This example shows a route from 1 to 16.

Now find the routes for these four grids.

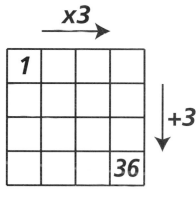

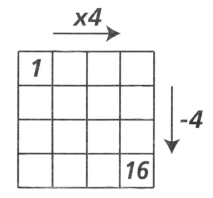

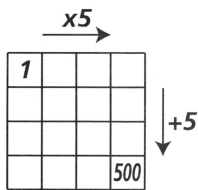

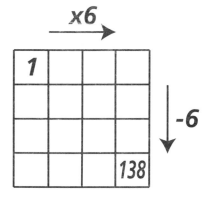

Twelve Factors

Amongst the numbers under 100 there are only five which have exactly twelve factors (including 1 and themselves).

List the factors of these numbers in the grid below.

Numbers in ascending order

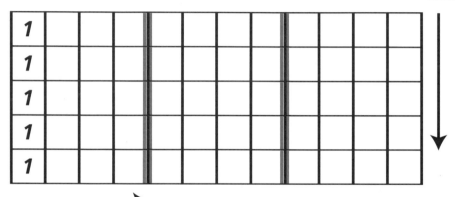

Factors in ascending order

One Way Only

The lists of twelve factors shown opposite can only be entered in this grid in one way.

The puzzle is to do so.

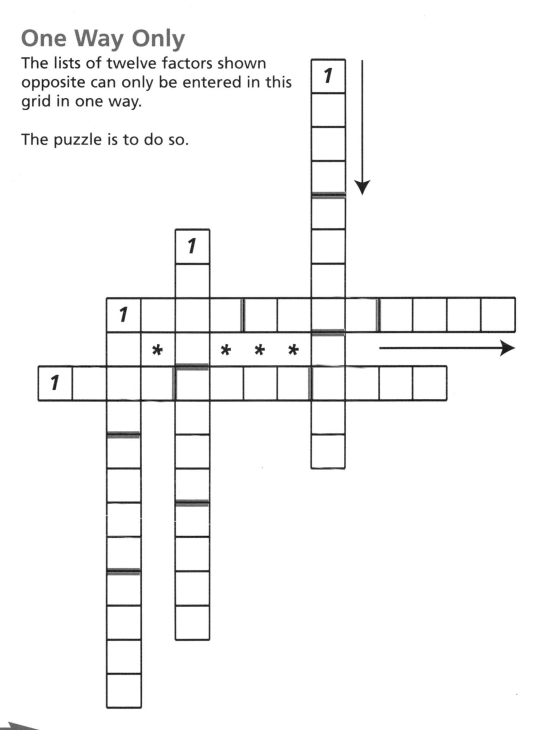

The Final Digit

Making a systematic investigation of number patterns means that it is sometimes possible to work out what the final digit of the result of a calculation must be even though the full answer is far too large to work out completely.

What is the final digit in each of these?

$$6^{127} \qquad 9^{128} \qquad 9^{129} \qquad 5^{130}$$

Using the experience so gained, calculate the final digit of the result of this sum.

$$2^{131} \quad \times \quad 3^{132}$$

Number Challenge 9

Plus and Minus Alternately

What is the sum of this sequence of numbers?

$$1 - 2 + 3 - 4 + 5 - 6 + \ldots + 2001 - 2002$$

And the sum of this sequence?

$$1 - 2 + 4 - 8 + 16 - 32 + \ldots + 1024$$

Number Challenge 10

Increasing Sums

In these addition sums, each number to be found is either 2 or 3 or 4 greater than the number in the previous box. In all cases the sum is 180.

Calculate what the number in each box has to be.

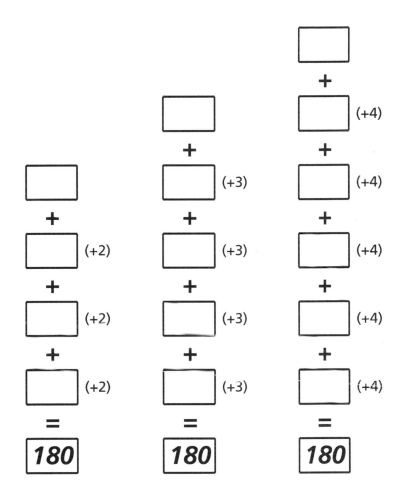

Number Challenge 11

Finding Averages

Each number in the middle of a row or column is the average of the numbers on either side of it.

Grid 1:

2		6
8	10	

Grid 2:

4	8	
14		22

Grid 3:

6		18
	26	32

Grid 4:

		24
17		
26		42

Grid 5:

10		30
32		52

Grid 6:

12		36
		49
38		

Grid 7:

14	28	
44		72

Grid 8:

16		48
	66	82

Grid 9:

18	36	54
56		92

Having completed the nine grids it is possible to check your answers by finding the average of all nine numbers in each square.

Can you now guess what is the average of all the numbers in all of the nine grids?

Lowest Common Factors

Complete this grid by entering into each of the eight squares the only common factor of the four numbers in the circles which surround it.

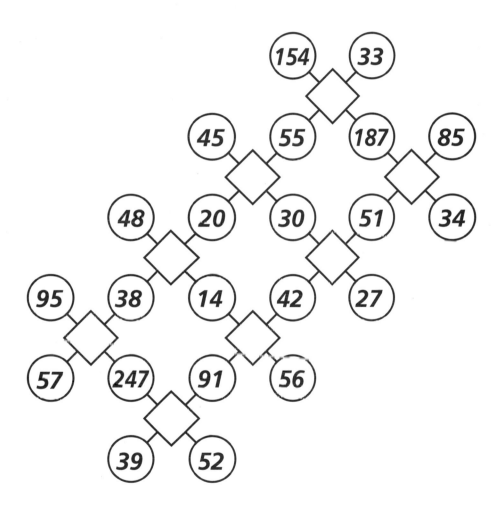

Now find a triangular number by dividing the sum of the two largest factors in the grid by the product of the two smallest.

Consecutive Primes

Each of these four subtraction sums leads to an answer which is a three-digit prime number.

It is also true that the four answers, placed in a suitable order, are consecutive primes.

The puzzle is to find them.

1	6	6	
–			6
=	6		

1		8	
–	8		8
=		8	

1		7	7
–	7	7	
=			

1			9
–	9	9	
=			9

4 x 4 Magic Squares

In this 4 x 4 Magic Square all the rows, columns and diagonals add up to 34 and all the numbers from 1 to 16 are used once each.

The first challenge is to complete the magic square.

			6
16	5	4	
	11		
	8		

1 2 3 7 9
10 12 13 14 15

Here is a list of the numbers which have not been used so far.

The next challenge is to complete this magic square.

This time use each of the first sixteen two-digit odd numbers, remembering that all the rows columns and diagonals must total the same.

33			
	37	17	39
		19	
		41	

Calendar Arithmetic

The first challenge here is to lay out the only possible calendar for January where the sum of the Saturday dates is a multiple of 17.

January

M	Tu	W	Th	F	Sa	Su

June

M	Tu	W	Th	F	Sa	Su

Now in the bottom grid lay out the only possible calendar for June where the sum of the Saturday dates is a multiple of 7.

Multiplication Squares

The nine digits 1, 2, 3, 4, 5, 6, 7, 8, 9 are entered into the cells of these 3 x 3 square grids exactly once each.

For both squares the results of multiplying the three numbers in each row or column together are given.
The challenge is to find the only possible way of assigning the digits to each of the grids.

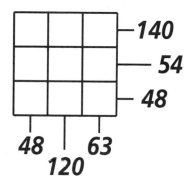

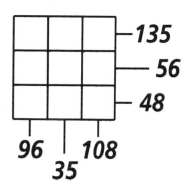

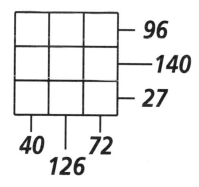

Horizontal Pattern Spotting

There is the same hidden relationship between the three
numbers in each of the three rows of these diagrams.

In each case discover what it is from the first two and then
use it to fill in the blank box.

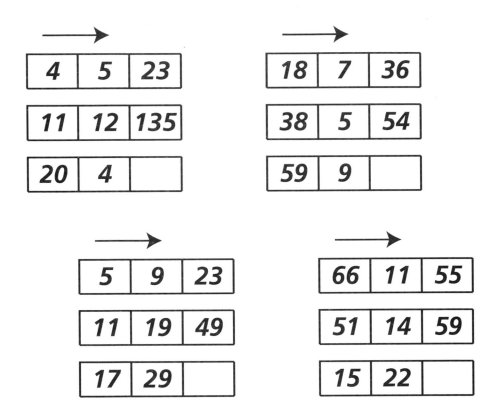

Operations Fill-ins

Fill in each of the blank squares with one of the operations, addition, subtraction, multiplication or division, so that all six equations become true.

5		**12**		**3**	**=**	**51**
	■		■		■	
16		**4**		**11**	**=**	**44**
	■		■		■	
7		**2**		**8**	**=**	**6**
=	■	**=**	■	**=**	■	
3		**4**		**41**		

To complete this first puzzle use what is called 'Polish Logic' where each operation is completed as you come to it.

For example

$$3 + 4 \times 5 = 35$$
and
$$35 - 14 \div 7 = 3.$$

To solve this puzzle use normal algebraic logic, where multiplication and division must be done before addition and subtraction.

For example

$$3 + 4 \times 5 = 23$$
and
$$35 - 14 \div 7 = 33.$$

3		**19**		**2**	**=**	**41**
	■		■		■	
6		**56**		**8**	**=**	**13**
	■		■		■	
8		**7**		**4**	**=**	**36**
=	■	**=**	■	**=**	■	
51		**11**		**34**		

Multiples of 66

Both of these four digit numbers can be divided exactly by 66 and conform to a pattern which may be written as xyyx.

2772   6336

The challenge is to find out how many other four digit numbers there are which can be divided by 66 and conform to the pattern xyyx.

Number Challenge 20

Digital Count

There are three times every day when a 24 hour digital clock shows only one digit.

These are midnight, 11.11(am) and 22.22(pm).

At 15.51, the display shows two different digits. The puzzle is to work out how many times during the 24 hour period the clock shows two different digits twice each.

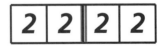

Common Factor Trails

Starting at each of the arrowed hexagons the idea is to cross from the top of each grid to the bottom.

Each move must be made from adjacent number to adjacent number but only moving between numbers which share a common factor apart from 1.

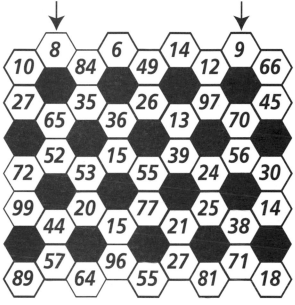

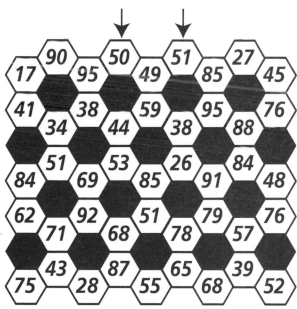

In all there are four trails to find, two in each diagram.

Number Challenge 22

Leaving out a Square

There are nine perfect squares between 0 and 100.

1,   4,   9,   16,   25,   36,   49,   64,   81

Arrange eight of them along the sides of this square grid so that the sum of each of the sides is as shown.
The position of 1 is given.

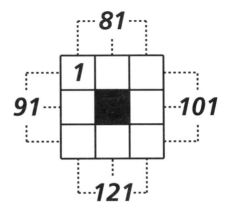

The same grid and the same puzzle but this time the 4 occupies the first position.
Discover where seven of the remaining square numbers go.

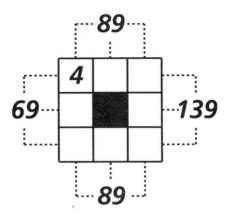

Number Challenge 23

Finite Sets

These six mystery numbers are strongly related to each other and when you find them you will know why there are no more. Such a set is known as a 'finite set'.

What are the six related numbers given that all their prime factors are shown below?
(Note: Prime factors can be repeated.)

Set of Related Numbers

3:5	***3:17***	***3:5:7***	***3:13***	***3:19***	***3:59***

Prime Factors of Related Numbers

Similarly what are the six numbers in this finite set?

Set of Related Numbers

2:3:13	***3***	***2:3***	***2:3:19***	***3:47***	***2:3***

Prime Factors of Related Numbers

What Colour

If this diagram with its pattern of white and orange boxes continues for ever, on what colour will each of the numbers listed below lie?

44

445

4446

1	2	3	4
5	6	7	8
9	10	11	12
13	14	15	16
17	18	19	20
21	22	23	24
25	26	27	28

If this second diagram also goes on for ever with its pattern of white, orange and grey boxes, on what colour will each of the numbers listed below lie?

75

776

7777

1	2	3	4
5	6	7	8
9	10	11	12
13	14	15	16
17	18	19	20
21	22	23	24
25	26	27	28

Number Challenge 25

Missing Integers

In this summation, one of the integers between 1 and 8 is missing, so there are not six integers as expected but five.

$$1 + . + . + . + . + . + 8 = 29$$

The total is therefore reduced from the expected 36.
Immediately it is obvious that the missing integer has to be 7.

$$1 + (only\ 5\ integers) + 8 = 29$$

Missing Integer is 7

Now find the missing integer in each of these summations.

$$1 + (only\ 7\ integers) + 10 = 50$$

$$1 + (only\ 10\ integers) + 13 = 80$$

$$1 + (only\ 17\ integers) + 20 = 197$$

$$1 + (only\ 22\ integers) + 25 = 306$$

When two integers are missing, the problem becomes more complicated.

$$1 + (only\ 26\ integers) + 30 = 441$$

What integers are missing from this summation?

There are a number of solutions but the pair of numbers required here are both prime and neither is a solution to the other puzzles on this page.

Hundred Masks

Each of the four masks below fits on this grid which shows the numbers 1 to 100. Which masks would leave the following sets of numbers showing?

1. Only Prime Numbers
2. Only Numbers divisible by 3
3. Only Multiples of 8
4. Only Numbers with 17 as a factor

1	2	3	4	5	6	7	8	9	10
11	12	13	14	15	16	17	18	19	20
21	22	23	24	25	26	27	28	29	30
31	32	33	34	35	36	37	38	39	40
41	42	43	44	45	46	47	48	49	50
51	52	53	54	55	56	57	58	59	60
61	62	63	64	65	66	67	68	69	70
71	72	73	74	75	76	77	78	79	80
81	82	83	84	85	86	87	88	89	90
91	92	93	94	95	96	97	98	99	100

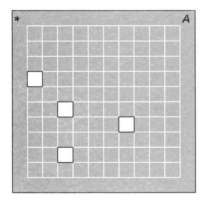

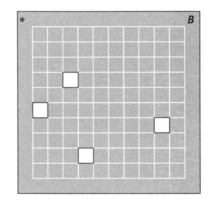

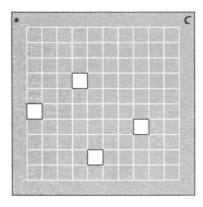

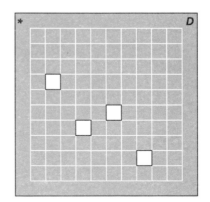

Number Fan Addition

Here are four number fans, with a number in each sector.

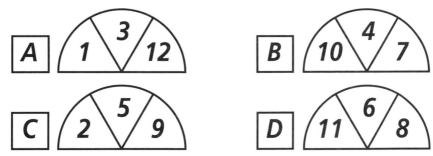

Corresponding sectors on the number fans are added together to give a new number fan. For example.

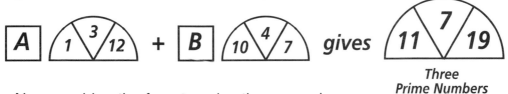

Three Prime Numbers

Now combine the fans to solve these puzzles.

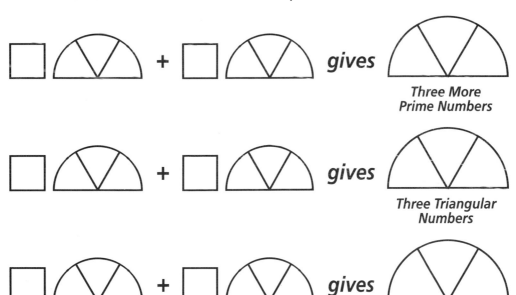

gives *Three More Prime Numbers*

gives *Three Triangular Numbers*

gives *Three Fibonacci Numbers*

Number Challenge 28

Sharing Factors

Here ten consecutive numbers are arranged in a circle showing dotted links between the lowest number and those with which it shares a common factor. (In addition to 1)

For example
60 & 62 share a factor of 2.
60 & 63 share a factor of 3.
60 & 64 share factors of 2 & 4.

Here are three further diagrams to fill in in a similar way starting with 70, 80 and 90.

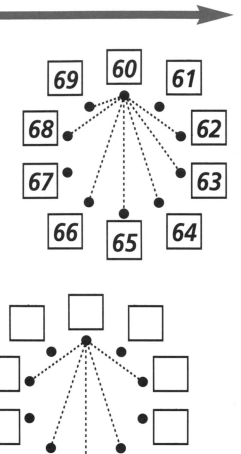

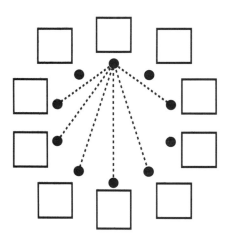

What would happen on similar diagrams for 40, 50 and 110?

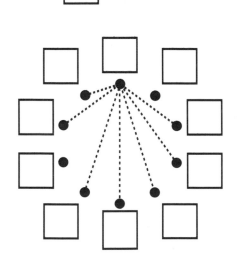

28

Magic Squares

Create four magic squares using the twelve rows given below.

In each magic square the rows, columns and diagonals all add up to the same total.

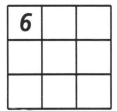
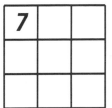

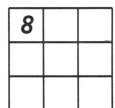
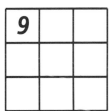

| 2 | 6 | 10 |

| 6 | 7 | 2 |

| 2 | 9 | 4 |

| 7 | 5 | 3 |

| 1 | 5 | 9 |

| 7 | 8 | 3 |

| 8 | 10 | 12 |

| 9 | 4 | 5 |

| 6 | 1 | 8 |

| 13 | 6 | 11 |

| 9 | 14 | 7 |

| 8 | 3 | 4 |

Reciprocal Fractions and Decimals

A pair of fractions like this is known as a reciprocal pair:

$$\frac{3}{8} \And \frac{8}{3}$$

They can also be expressed in decimal form:

$$\frac{3}{8} = 0.375 \And \frac{8}{3} = 2.66666\ldots$$

In one case the decimal terminates and in the other it carries on for ever.

The challenge here is to look for all the reciprocal pairs, using the numbers 1 to 100, where both decimals terminate.

First there are those where one of the numbers is 1.

$$\frac{1}{8} \And \frac{8}{1}$$

How many of these are there?

Now find the rest; there are only twelve more.

Shared Factors

These four-digit numbers all share the same two-digit factor.
Fill in the squares below to show what it is.

$1608 =$ ☐☐ x

$3015 =$ ☐☐ x $\Big\}$ ☐☐

$4690 =$ ☐☐ x

Similarly these five-digit numbers all share the same three-digit factor. Fill in the squares below to show what it is.

$58338 =$ ☐☐☐ x

$64820 =$ ☐☐☐ x

$76395 =$ ☐☐☐ x $\Big\}$ ☐☐☐

$97230 =$ ☐☐☐ x

Digital Cascades

In the top row of this diagram are the digits 1, 2, 3, 4, 5 and below each pair of digits is their sum. However if the sum has more than one digit those digits are added together to give a single digit. This process can be repeated, working in pairs, until, in the fifth row, the result is a single digit.

This whole process is called a 'digital cascade'.

Use the digits 1 to 9 to complete these digital cascades.

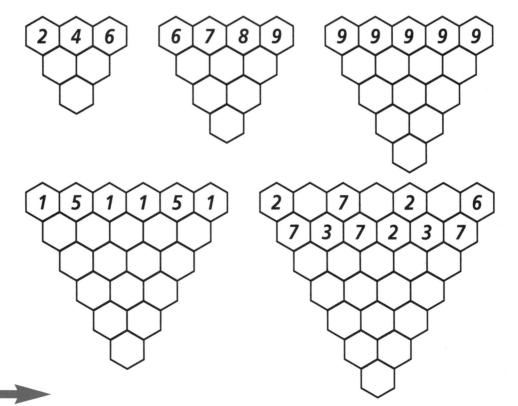

More Digital Cascades

Complete this diagram by entering the successive digital roots of each pair of numbers until the final digit of 9 is reached.

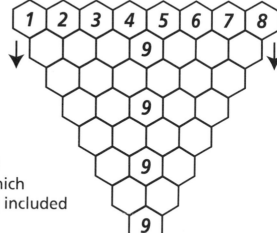

You will see that the digit 9 occurs exactly four times which is one ninth of the 36 digits included in this diagram.

Now find out which of the digits 1 to 8 occurs most often.

This extract from the cascade above shows the three-digit number producing a final digit root of 8 via the number 26.

There are eight more three-digit numbers which have this property. The challenge is to find all eight of them.

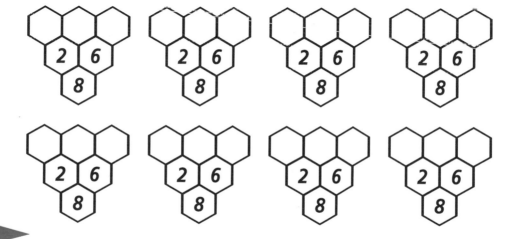

Number Challenge 34

Sums of Squares

The squares of certain numbers are the sum of two other squares. The best known such example is

$$5^2 = 4^2 + 3^2$$

These five numbers have the same property.
Complete these patterns.

$$10^2 = \square^2 + \square^2 \qquad 13^2 = \square^2 + \square^2$$

$$15^2 = \square^2 + \square^2 \qquad 17^2 = \square^2 + \square^2$$

$$20^2 = \square^2 + \square^2$$

The number 25 can be reached in two different ways.
Find both.

$$25^2 = \square^2 + \square^2 \qquad 25^2 = \square^2 + \square^2$$

The number 65 can be reached in four different ways.
Find all four.

$$65^2 = \square^2 + \square^2 \qquad 65^2 = \square^2 + \square^2$$

$$65^2 = \square^2 + \square^2 \qquad 65^2 = \square^2 + \square^2$$

Squares from 1 to 40 are given on page 48.
For squares from 41 to 65 see opposite.

Almost the Same Sum

Because there is an odd number of odd numbers in this set of eight numbers we can be certain that they cannot be divided into two sets with the same sum.

9, 18, 69, 7, 48, 22, 30, 26

The challenge is to divide them into two sets where the difference between the sums of those sets is as small as possible.

Now divide this second set of numbers into two sets whose sums are also as close together as possible.

26, 46, 5, 30, 18, 84, 16, 60

This time there are two different ways which are equally close.

	Square		Square		Square		Square		Square
41	1681	46	2116	51	2601	56	3136	61	3721
42	1764	47	2209	52	2704	57	3249	62	3844
43	1849	48	2304	53	2809	58	3364	63	3969
44	1936	49	2401	54	2916	59	3481	64	4096
45	2025	50	2500	55	3025	60	3600	65	4225

Which is Larger?

With the aid of calculators and computers it is now possible to work out and therefore compare very large numbers indeed.

However, for these challenges, the puzzle is to work out which is the larger number of a pair without ever working out the actual value of the numbers.

A. 2^{350} & 5^{150}

B. 7^{144} & 19^{96}

C. 3^{108} & 9^{54}

D. 10^{30} & 2^{100}

E. 11^{99} & 6^{132}

Number Challenge 37

Adding Primes

The numbers needed to complete this magic square are all primes. The central number is 37 and therefore we know that all rows, columns and diagonals must add up to 111.

Find all the other entries.

1	37	

Large and Small Factors

Each of the four numbers below is larger than a million.
Interestingly they all have one four-digit prime factor and lots
of one-digit ones. The challenge is to discover the large
factor in each case.

1336860 ☐☐☐☐

1073016 ☐☐☐☐

1607025 ☐☐☐☐

1560762 ☐☐☐☐

The Millionth Decimal Place

If the nine digits 1, 2, 3, 4, 5, 6, 7, 8, 9 are repeated endlessly
to form an infinite decimal then it is not too hard to work out
that the millionth decimal place is occupied by the digit 1.

0.123456789 ...

A much more interesting challenge is to discover which digit
occupies the millionth decimal place if the infinite decimal is
constructed according to this pattern.

0.123456789101112131415 ...

Fibonacci Squares

Each term in the Fibonacci sequence of numbers is the sum of the two previous terms. It can be generated by starting with the two terms 0 and 1.

$$0, 1, 1, 2, 3, 5, 8, ...$$

It is usual to ignore the leading zero and so the first twelve Fibonacci numbers are

$$1, 1, 2, 3, 5, 8, 13, 21, 34, 55, 89, 144, ...$$

A curious and interesting property of Fibonacci numbers arises from the sum of their squares.

$$1^2 = 1 = 1 \times 1$$
$$1^2 + 1^2 = 2 = 1 \times 2$$
$$1^2 + 1^2 + 2^2 = 6 = 2 \times 3$$
$$1^2 + 1^2 + 2^2 + 3^2 = 15 = 3 \times 5$$

The challenge is to work out the sum of the first twelve Fibonacci squares without actually summing them.

$$1^2 + 1^2 + 2^2 + ... + 144^2 = ?$$

Now find how many consecutive squares of Fibonacci numbers are needed for their sum to exceed a million for the first time.

38

Odd Squares and Odd Cubes

If odd numbers are added together in this kind of way then their totals are perfect squares:

$$1 = 1$$
$$1 + 3 = 4$$
$$1 + 3 + 5 = 9$$
$$1 + 3 + 5 + 7 = 16$$
$$1 + 3 + 5 + 7 + 9 = 25$$
$$1 + 3 + 5 + 7 + 9 + 11 = 36$$

and so on

$$1 + \text{.....................} + 99 = 2500 = 50^2$$

Whereas if they are added together in this kind of way then their totals are perfect cubes:

$$1 = 1$$
$$3 + 5 = 8$$
$$7 + 9 + 11 = 27$$
$$13 + 15 + 17 + 19 = 64$$
$$21 + 23 + 25 + 27 + 29 = 125$$

and so on

$$? + \text{.....................} + ? = 125\,000 = 50^3$$

The puzzle is to work out how many odd numbers it contains and where this final line begins and ends.

Guessing Cube Roots

If a large number is known to be a perfect cube then, by a series of logical guesses, it is possible to work out what number it is the cube of. In other words, to arrive at the cube root of such a number.

$$1^3 = 1, \qquad 2^3 = 8, \qquad 3^3 = 27, \qquad 4^3 = 64,$$

$$5^3 = 125, \quad 6^3 = 216, \quad 7^3 = 343, \quad 8^3 = 512,$$

$$9^3 = 729, \quad 10^3 = 1000$$

It is a curious fact that the cubes of the single digits 0 to 9 end with the digits 0 to 9, but not in the same order. Therefore the final digit of a perfect cube offers an important clue as to what the cube root must be. There are also other clues which you can get from the list above.

This challenge is to use logical guesswork to find the cube root of each of the six numbers shown below.

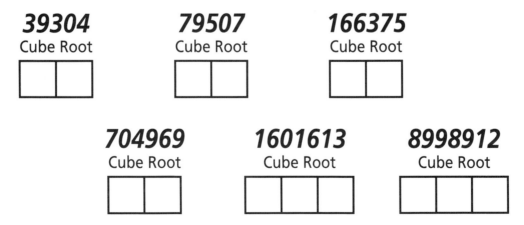

39304
Cube Root

79507
Cube Root

166375
Cube Root

704969
Cube Root

1601613
Cube Root

8998912
Cube Root

Remember that there are other clues which you can get from the list of cubes at the top of the page.

Cross Out Two

Cross out two of the numbers in this 4 x 4 square so that all the rows and columns add up to multiples of 4.

8	9	5	2
3	9	7	5
4	6	2	8
9	8	5	6

Cross out two of the numbers in this 4 x 4 square so that all the rows and columns add up to multiples of 3.

2	7	8	4
5	9	1	3
4	6	5	2
4	5	6	8

Number Challenge 44

Consecutive Numbers

Which sets of six consecutive numbers fit into these two sets of boxes so that they have the given properties?

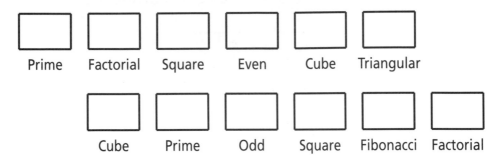

Prime	Factorial	Square	Even	Cube	Triangular

Cube	Prime	Odd	Square	Fibonacci	Factorial

Number Challenge 45

Nines

It is easy to tell if any number is divisible by 9. Simply add the digits together and see if their sum is divisible by 9.

8	9		2	3		7	3		9	6		4	8

The five two-digit tiles above will fit into the gaps in the four six-digit numbers below.

The challenge is to fit four of the five tiles into the gaps so that each six-digit number is divisible by 9.

6	8			2	6	4	7	5			5

3			9	2	1	7	8	2	0		

Elevens

To test if a number is divisible by 11, add each of the sets of alternate digits together. If the two totals are equal or differ by a multiple of 11, the original number is divisible by 11.

Here are two examples

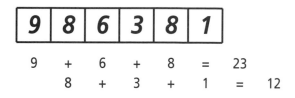

9	**8**	**6**	**3**	**8**	**1**

9 + 6 + 8 = 23
8 + 3 + 1 = 12

4	**8**	**6**	**7**	**9**	**4**

4 + 6 + 9 = 19
8 + 7 + 4 = 19

Both 986 381 and 486 794 are divisible by 11.

9	**2**		**7**	**9**		**6**	**5**		**4**	**8**		**3**	**0**

The five two-digit tiles above will fit into the gaps in the four six-digit numbers below.
The challenge is to fit four of the five tiles into the gaps so that each six-digit number is divisible by 11.

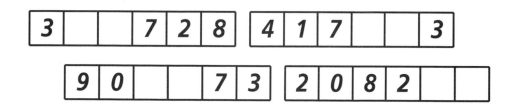

3			**7**	**2**	**8**		**4**	**1**	**7**			**3**

9	**0**			**7**	**3**		**2**	**0**	**8**	**2**		

43

Between the Squares

This challenge concerns pairs of consecutive squares and any integer that lies between them.

Take for example the consecutive squares 121 and 144 and the integer 126.

$$\boxed{126} - \left(\boxed{5} \ x \ \boxed{18} \right) = \boxed{36}$$

Integer   Difference   Difference   Perfect
between   between   Square
lower square   upper square
and integer   and integer

It is a provable fact that:
Taking any integer which lies between two consecutive perfect squares, the result of subtracting the product of the differences between that integer and the two squares from the integer itself is always a perfect square.
The result above is 36 the square of 6.

121 144

The challenge is to find two numbers between 121 and 144 which produce the square of 9.

169 196

And now looking at the consecutive squares 169 and 196 and the integers between them. Which ones produce the square of 1 when treated in the same way?

Each Digit Twice

All of these six-digit numbers have the property that each includes just three different digits.
Complete the empty squares according to the divisibility rules.

(a) These three numbers are all exactly divisible by 13.

| 2 | 5 | 8 | | | |

| 4 | 7 | 1 | | | |

| 6 | 9 | 3 | | | |

(b) These six numbers have 11 as a factor.

| 3 | 5 | 9 | | | | | 3 | 5 | 9 | | | |

| 7 | 4 | 6 | | | | | 7 | 4 | 6 | | | |

| 8 | 2 | 1 | | | | | 8 | 2 | 1 | | | |

(c) These three numbers are all multiples of 7.

| 1 | 4 | 2 | | | |

| 3 | 6 | 7 | | | |

| 5 | 9 | 8 | | | |

Can you see the reason why the answers turn out as they do?

Number Challenge 49

Binary Addition

The binary system of numbers uses only 0 and 1 as symbols.
The table below shows how the sequence develops.

(1)	(2,3)	(4 to 7)	(8 to 15)	(16 to 31)	(32 to 63)
1	**10**	**100**	**1000**	**10000**	**100000**
	11	**101**	**1001**	**10001**	**100001**
		110	**1010**	**10010**	**100010**
		111	**1011**	And so on through all 5 digit numbers as far as	And so on through all 6 digit numbers as far as
			1100		
			1101		
			1110	**11111**	**111111**
			1111		

Number Bonds for Binary Arithmetic

$$0 + 0 = 0 \quad 0 + 1 = 1 \quad 1 + 0 = 1 \quad 1 + 1 = 10$$

The challenge here is to complete the following additions
using binary numbers as well as in the usual Base 10 notation.

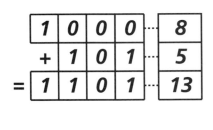

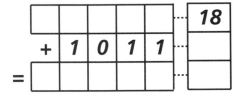

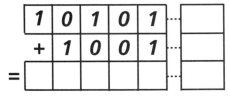

46

Antimagic Squares

The only magic square using the digits 1 to 9 is well known and is called "Lo Shu'.

8	1	6
3	5	7
4	9	2

All the rows columns and diagonals add up to 15.

An antimagic square is one where all the rows, columns and diagonals add up to different totals.

The challenge is to complete the squares below using the digits 1 to 9 once each. In each case the totals for the three rows, the three columns and the two diagonals are given.

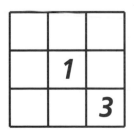

Row totals: 6, 18, 21
Column totals: 12, 16, 17
Diagonal totals: 15, 19

Row totals: 11, 14, 20
Column totals: 8, 16, 21
Diagonal totals: 12, 17

Prime Numbers

2	101	211	307	401	503	601	701	809	907
3	103	223	311	409	509	607	709	811	911
5	107	227	313	419	521	613	719	821	919
7	109	229	317	421	523	617	727	823	929
11	113	233	331	431	541	619	733	827	937
13	127	239	337	433	547	631	739	829	941
17	131	241	347	439	557	641	743	839	947
19	137	251	349	443	563	643	751	853	953
23	139	257	353	449	569	647	757	857	967
29	149	263	359	457	571	653	761	859	971
31	151	269	367	461	577	659	769	863	977
37	157	271	373	463	587	661	773	877	983
41	163	277	379	467	593	673	787	881	991
43	167	281	383	479	599	677	797	883	997
47	173	283	389	487		683		887	
53	179	293	397	491		691			
59	181			499					
61	191								
67	193								
71	197								
73	199								
79									
83									
89									
97									

Squares & Cubes

	Square	Cube		Square	Cube
1	1	1	21	441	9261
2	4	8	22	484	10648
3	9	27	23	529	12167
4	16	64	24	576	13824
5	25	125	25	625	15625
6	36	216	26	676	17576
7	49	343	27	729	19683
8	64	512	28	784	21952
9	81	729	29	841	24389
10	100	1000	30	900	27000
11	121	1331	31	961	29791
12	144	1728	32	1024	32768
13	169	2197	33	1089	35937
14	196	2744	34	1156	39304
15	225	3375	35	1225	42875
16	256	4096	36	1296	46656
17	289	4913	37	1369	50653
18	324	5832	38	1444	54872
19	361	6859	39	1521	59319
20	400	8000	40	1600	64000

Triangular Numbers

1	190	703
3	210	741
6	231	780
10	253	820
15	276	861
21	300	903
28	325	946
36	351	990
45	378	
55	406	
66	435	
78	465	
91	496	
105	528	
120	561	
136	595	
153	630	
171	666	

Proper Factors

4	2									
6	2	3								
8	2	4								
9	3									
10	2	5								
12	2	3	4	6						
14	2	7								
15	3	5								
16	2	4	8							
18	2	3	6	9						
20	2	4	5	10						
21	3	7								
22	2	11								
24	2	3	4	6	8	12				
25	5									
26	2	13								
27	3	9								
28	2	4	7	14						
30	2	3	5	6	10	15				
32	2	4	8	16						
33	3	11								
34	2	17								
35	5	7								
36	2	3	4	6	9	12	18			
38	2	19								
39	3	13								
40	2	4	5	8	10	20				
42	2	3	6	7	14	21				
44	2	4	11	22						
45	3	5	9	15						
46	2	23								
48	2	3	4	6	8	12	16	24		
49	7									
50	2	5	10	25						
51	3	17								
52	2	4	13	26						
54	2	3	6	9	18	27				
55	5	11								
56	2	4	7	8	14	28				
57	3	19								
58	2	29								
60	2	3	4	5	6	10	12	15	20	30
62	2	31								
63	3	7	9	21						
64	2	4	8	16	32					
65	5	13								
66	2	3	6	11	22	33				
68	2	4	17	34						
69	3	23								
70	2	5	7	10	14	35				
72	2	3	4	6	8	9	12	18	24	36
74	2	37								
75	3	5	15	25						
76	2	4	19	38						
77	7	11								
78	2	3	6	13	26	39				
80	2	4	5	8	10	16	20	40		
81	3	9	27							
82	2	41								
84	2	3	4	6	7	12	14	21	28	42
85	5	17								
86	2	43								
87	3	29								
88	2	4	8	11	22	44				
90	2	3	5	6	9	10	15	18	30	45
91	7	13								
92	2	4	23	46						
93	3	31								
94	2	47								
95	5	19								
96	2	3	4	6	8	12	16	24	32	48
98	2	7	14	49						
99	3	9	11	33						
100	2	4	5	10	20	25	50			

Factorials

1!	1
2!	2
3!	6
4!	24
5!	120
6!	720
7!	5040
8!	40 320
9!	362 880
10!	39 916 800

Fibonacci Numbers

1	89
1	144
2	233
3	377
5	610
8	987
13	1597
21	2584
34	4181
55	6765

Answers 1 to 6

Number Challenge 1

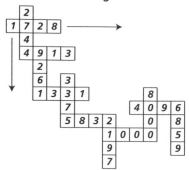

Number Challenge 4

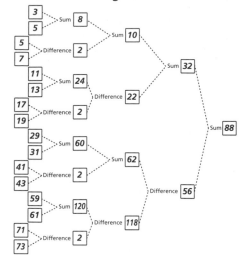

Number Challenge 2

For this kind of puzzle it is necessary to spot the hidden relationship. Some may prefer to express this relationship in algebraic terms, others as working with a pattern of numbers.

4 x 5 x 9
4ab

2	3	5
11	7	9
88	84	180

167 - 48 + 1
a - b + 1

35	45	167
17	22	48
19	24	120

(9 + 1)(7 + 1)
(a + 1)(b + 1)

7	11	9
11	6	7
96	84	80

(266 ÷ 7) + 2
(a ÷ b) + 2

91	51	266
13	17	7
9	5	40

Number Challenge 5
The only routes are these.

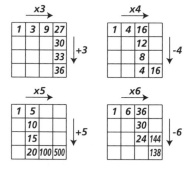

x3

1	3	9	27
			30
			33
			36

+3

x4

1	4	16
		12
		8
	4	16

-4

x5

1	5		
10			
15			
20	100	500	

+5

x6

1	6	36
		30
	24	144
		138

-6

Number Challenge 3

12	1	18
9	6	4
2	36	3

These squares may also be reflected about a vertical axis.

28	1	98
49	14	4
2	196	7

75	1	45
9	15	25
5	225	3

Number Challenge 6
The only five numbers under 100 with exactly 12 factors are 60, 72, 84, 90, 96.

1	2	3	4	5	6	10	12	15	20	30	60
1	2	3	4	6	8	9	12	18	24	36	72
1	2	3	4	6	7	12	14	21	28	42	84
1	2	3	5	6	9	10	15	18	30	45	90
1	2	3	4	6	8	12	16	24	32	48	96

Number Challenge 7

Count the number of squares to the crossing points in each line of the grid and then use the chart on page 8 to decide which must go where.

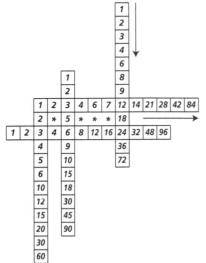

Number Challenge 8

$6^1 = 6$, $6^2 = 36$, $6^3 = 216$, so all powers of 6 must end in a 6.

$\therefore 6^{127}$ ends with 6.

$9^1 = 9$, $9^2 = 81$, $9^3 = 729$, so powers of 9 must end with a 1 or a 9 according to whether the power is even or odd.

$\therefore 9^{128}$ ends with 1. $\therefore 9^{129}$ ends with 9.

All powers of 5 end in a 5.

$\therefore 5^{130}$ ends with 5.

$2^{131} \times 3^{132} = 6^{131} \times 3$.

$\therefore 2^{131} \times 3^{132}$ must end with an 8.

Number Challenge 9

The first sequence groups into pairs.

$(1 - 2 = -1, 3 - 4 = -1, \quad 2001 - 2002 = -1)$

$\therefore -1 \times 1001 = -1001$

For the second series let S be its sum.

$\therefore S = 1 - 2 + 4 - 8 + 16 \quad + 1024$

and $2S = 2 - 4 + 8 - 16 \quad - 1024 + 2048$

$\therefore 3S = 1 + 2048 = 2049 \therefore S = 683$

Number Challenge 10

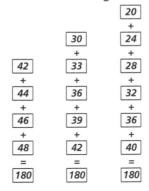

Number Challenge 11

2	4	6
5	7	9
8	10	12

4	8	12
9	13	17
14	18	22

6	12	18
13	19	25
20	26	32

8	16	24
17	25	33
26	34	42

10	20	30
21	31	41
32	42	52

12	24	36
25	37	49
38	50	62

14	28	42
29	43	57
44	58	72

16	32	48
33	49	65
50	66	82

18	36	54
37	55	73
56	74	92

The average of all nine numbers is the same as the one at the centre. Yes, 31 because the centre numbers also form an arithmetic progression.

Number Challenge 12

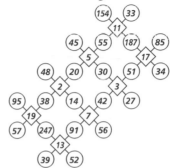

The triangular number is 6.

$(17 + 19) \div (2 \times 3)$

Number Challenge 13

Consulting the list on page 48, there are only two possible groups of four prime numbers which could satisfy the digits which are given.

Either 587, 593, 599, 601

Or 683, 691, 701, 709.

Trial and error will eliminate the first group.

```
  1 6 6 7
-   9 7 6
= 6 9 1
```

```
  1 4 7 7
-   7 7 6
= 7 0 1
```

```
  1 5 8 1
-   8 9 8
= 6 8 3
```

```
  1 6 9 9
-   9 9 0
= 7 0 9
```

Number Challenge 14

For the second example it is first necessary to work out what each line should add up to. The numbers are 11 to 41 and the sum of all 16 is 416. Hence each row of 4 must add up to 104.

3	10	15	6
16	5	4	9
2	11	14	7
13	8	1	12

33	23	27	21
11	37	17	39
25	31	19	29
35	13	41	15

Number Challenge 15

January

M	Tu	W	Th	F	Sa	Su
				1	2	3	4
5	6	7	8	9	10	11
12	13	14	15	16	17	18
19	20	21	22	23	24	25
26	27	28	29	30	31	

June

M	Tu	W	Th	F	Sa	Su
						1
2	3	4	5	6	7	8
9	10	11	12	13	14	15
16	17	18	19	20	21	22
23	24	25	26	27	28	29
30						

Number Challenge 16

The third puzzle has two solutions because 2 x 9 = 6 x 3.

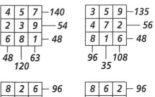

```
4 5 7 —140      3 5 9 —135
2 3 9 — 54      4 7 2 — 56
6 8 1 — 48      8 1 6 — 48
48  63          96  108
   120             35
```

```
8 2 6 — 96      8 6 2 — 96
5 7 4 —140      5 7 4 —140
1 9 3 — 27      1 3 9 — 27
40  72          40  72
  126             126
```

Number Challenge 17

The four patterns are as follows.

→		
4	5	23
11	12	135
20	4	83

20 x 4 + 3
ab + 3

→		
18	7	36
38	5	54
59	9	79

59 + 9 + 11
a + b + 11

→		
5	9	23
11	19	49
17	29	75

17 + (2 x 29)
a + 2b

→		
66	11	55
51	14	59
15	22	71

(15 ÷ 3) + (3 x 22)
(a ÷ 3) + 3b

Number Challenge 18

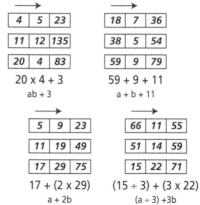

```
5 + 12 x 3 = 51        3 + 19 x 2 = 41
+   -    x             +   -    +
16 ÷ 4 x 11 = 44       6 + 56 ÷ 8 = 13
÷   ÷    +             x   ÷    x
7 x 2 - 8 = 6          8 + 7 x 4 = 36
=   =    =             =   =    =
3   4   41             51  11   34
```

Number Challenge 19

x must be even and x + y must be divisible by 3.

There are 11 more such numbers :

2112, 2442, 4224, 4554, 4884, 6006, 6666, 6996, 8118, 8448, 8778.

Number Challenge 20

There are 49 times when two digits occur twice each:

0011, 0022, 0033, 0044, 0055,
0101, 0110, 0202, 0220, 0303,
0330, 0404, 0440, 0505, 0550,
0606, 0707, 0808, 0909, 1001,
1010, 1100, 1122, 1133, 1144,
1155, 1212, 1221, 1313, 1331,
1414, 1441, 1515, 1551, 1616,
1717, 1818, 1919, 2002, 2020,
2112, 2121, 2200, 2211, 2233,
2244, 2255, 2323, 2332.

Number Challenge 21

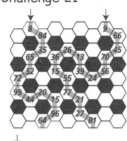

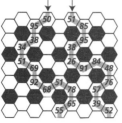

Number Challenge 22

Number Challenge 23

Set of Related Numbers

135	153	315	351	513	531
3:5	3:17	3:5:7	3:13	3:19	3:59

Prime Factors of Related Numbers

Set of Related Numbers

234	243	324	342	423	432
2:3:13	3	2:3	2:3:19	3:47	2:3

Prime Factors of Related Numbers

Number Challenge 24

44: orange, 445: orange, 4446: white. The pattern repeats every 16 numbers, so divide by 16 to determine the remainder.

75: white, 776: orange, 7777: grey. The complete pattern repeats every 48 numbers, so divide by 48 to get the remainder.

Number Challenge 25

The sum of the first n integers is n(n+1)/2. Knowing what the total should be identifies which number or numbers are missing.
5, 11, 13, 19
7 & 17

Number Challenge 26

1. A: 31, 53, 67, 83
2. B: 33, 51, 69, 84
3. D: 32, 56, 64, 88
4. C: 34, 51, 68, 85

Number Challenge 27

Three More Prime Numbers

Three Triangular Numbers

Three Fibonacci Numbers

Number Challenge 28

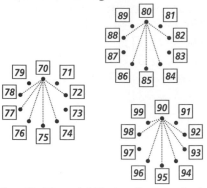

For 40, 50 and 110 the diagram is the same as for 80.

Number Challenge 29

Of the twelve rows given, six add up to 15, three to 18 and three to 30. This means that two squares have a 5 in the central position, one a 6 and one a 10. From then on it is a question of trial and error.

6	1	8
7	5	3
2	9	4

7	8	3
2	6	10
9	4	5

8	3	4
1	5	9
6	7	2

9	14	7
8	10	12
13	6	11

Number Challenge 30

There are 14 pairs:
1/2 & 2/1, 1/4 & 4/1, 1/5 & 5/1, 1/8 & 8/1, 1/10 & 10/1, 1/16 & 16/1, 1/20 & 20/1, 1/25 & 25/1, 1/32 & 32/1, 1/40 & 40/1, 1/50 & 50/1, 1/64 & 64/1, 1/100 & 100/1.

The twelve pairs are:
2/5 & 5/2, 2/25 & 25/2, 4/5 & 5/4, 4/25 & 25/4, 8/5 & 5/8, 8/25 & 25/8, 16/5 & 5/16, 16/25 & 25/16, 32/5 & 5/32, 25/32 & 32/25, 64/5 & 5/64, 64/25 & 25/64.

Number Challenge 31

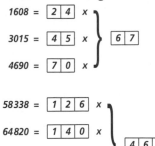

$$1608 = \boxed{2\ 4} \times$$
$$3015 = \boxed{4\ 5} \times \Bigg\} \boxed{6\ 7}$$
$$4690 = \boxed{7\ 0} \times$$

$$58338 = \boxed{1\ 2\ 6} \times$$
$$64820 = \boxed{1\ 4\ 0} \times \Bigg\} \boxed{4\ 6\ 3}$$
$$76395 = \boxed{1\ 6\ 5} \times$$
$$97230 = \boxed{2\ 1\ 0} \times$$

Number Challenge 32

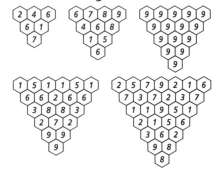

Number Challenge 33

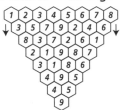

Each of the nine digits occurs four times.

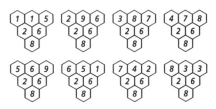

Number Challenge 34

$$\boxed{10}^2 = \boxed{8}^2 + \boxed{6}^2 \qquad \boxed{13}^2 = \boxed{12}^2 + \boxed{5}^2$$

$$\boxed{15}^2 = \boxed{12}^2 + \boxed{9}^2 \qquad \boxed{17}^2 = \boxed{15}^2 + \boxed{8}^2$$

$$\boxed{20}^2 = \boxed{16}^2 + \boxed{12}^2$$

$$\boxed{25}^2 = \boxed{24}^2 + \boxed{7}^2 \qquad \boxed{25}^2 = \boxed{20}^2 + \boxed{15}^2$$

$$\boxed{65}^2 = \boxed{63}^2 + \boxed{16}^2 \qquad \boxed{65}^2 = \boxed{60}^2 + \boxed{25}^2$$

$$\boxed{65}^2 = \boxed{56}^2 + \boxed{33}^2 \qquad \boxed{65}^2 = \boxed{52}^2 + \boxed{39}^2$$

Number Challenge 35

The sum of all eight numbers is 229, so what are needed are the nearest two possible totals to 114.5. Try 114 & 115
This is possible so the solutions are:
115 (69, 30, 9, 7) & 114 (48, 26, 22, 18)
The sum of all eight numbers is 285, so what are needed are the nearest two possible totals to 142.5.
143 &142 are not possible, so the two next best solutions are:
144 (84, 26, 18, 16) & 141 (60, 46, 30, 5)
144 (84, 60) & 141 (46, 30, 26, 18, 16, 5)

Number Challenge 36

A: 2^{350}
Because $(2^7)^{50}$ is greater than $(5^3)^{50}$
B: 19^{96}
Because $(19^2)^{48}$ is greater than $(7^3)^{48}$
C: Equal
Because $(3^2)^{54} = (9)^{54}$
D: 2^{100}
Because $(2^{10})^{10}$ is greater than $(10^3)^{10}$
E: 11^{99}
Because $(11^3)^{33}$ is greater than $(6^4)^{33}$

Number Challenge 37

67	13	31		43	61	7
1	37	73		1	37	73
43	61	7		67	13	31

The numbers can be arranged in two different ways.

But these answers are really the same.
One solution is a reflection of the other.

Number Challenge 38

Use successive division to remove smaller factors.

1336860 [1 0 6 1]
   1073016 [2 1 2 9]
      1607025 [3 0 6 1]
         1560762 [4 1 2 9]

Number Challenge 39

In the example $10^9 \div 9 = 111\,111$ rem 1.

To solve the challenge count the digits in a systematic way:
Single digit: 1 to 9 = 9 x 1 = 9
Two digits: 10 to 99 = 90 x 2 = 180
Three digits: 100 to 999 = 900 x 3 = 2700
Four digits:
1000 to 9999 = 9000 x 4 = 36 000
Five digits:
10 000 to 99 999 = 90 000 x 5 = 145 000
Six digits:
100 000 to 185 184 = 85 185 x 6 = 511 110
The total so far amounts to 999 999 digits, so the millionth is the first digit of the next number 185185, namely 1.

Number Challenge 40

33 552 (144 x 233)
The product of the 16th and 17th Fibonacci numbers is the first such product to exceed one million
Hence 16 (987 x 1597)

Number Challenge 41

There must be 50 consecutive odd numbers with an average value of 2500. Hence the first term is 2451 and the last term 2549.

Number Challenge 42

39304	79507	166375
Cube Root	Cube Root	Cube Root
[3 4]	[4 3]	[5 5]

704969	1601613	8998912
Cube Root	Cube Root	Cube Root
[8 9]	[1 1 7]	[2 0 8]

Number Challenge 43

8	9	5	2
3	9	■	■
4	6	2	8
9	8	5	6

2	7	8	4
5	9	1	3
4	6	■	2
4	5	6	■

Number Challenge 44

23	24	25	26	27	28
Prime	Factorial	Square	Even	Cube	Triangular

1	2	3	4	5	6
Cube	Prime	Odd	Square	Fibonacci	Factorial

Number Challenge 45

| 8 | 9 | | 2 | 3 | | 7 | 3 | | 9 | 6 | | 4 | 8 |

| 6 | 8 | 2 | 3 | 2 | 6 | 4 | 7 | 5 | 9 | 6 | 5 |

| 3 | 4 | 8 | 9 | 2 | 1 | 7 | 8 | 2 | 0 | 7 | 3 |

Number Challenge 46

| 9 | 2 | | 7 | 9 | | 6 | 5 | | 4 | 8 | | 3 | 0 |

| 3 | 6 | 5 | 7 | 2 | 8 | 4 | 1 | 7 | 9 | 2 | 3 |

| 9 | 0 | 7 | 9 | 7 | 3 | 2 | 0 | 8 | 2 | 3 | 0 |

Number Challenge 47

Use trial and error
123 & 142
181 & 183

Number Challenge 48

It is a significant fact that
7 x 11 x 13 = 1001.

2	5	8	2	5	8
4	7	1	4	7	1
6	9	3	6	9	3

3	5	9	3	5	9
7	4	6	7	4	6
8	2	1	8	2	1

3	5	9	9	5	3
7	4	6	6	4	7
8	2	1	1	2	8

1	4	2	1	4	2
3	6	7	3	6	7
5	9	8	5	9	8

Number Challenge 49

	1	0	0	1	0	18
+	1	0	1	1		11
=	1	1	1	0	1	29

	1	0	1	0	1	21
+	1	0	0	1		9
=	1	1	1	1	0	30

	1	0	1	0	0	1	41
+	1	0	0	1	1		19
=	1	1	1	1	0	0	60

Number Challenge 50

1	2	3
8	9	4
7	6	5

8	5	7
4	1	6
9	2	3

If you have enjoyed this book there may be other Tarquin books which would interest you, including 'The Number Detective' by Jon Millington and 'The Number Puzzler' by Roy Mullins. Tarquin books are available from bookshops, toy shops and gift shops or in case of difficulty, directly by post from the publishers.
See our full range of books on our secure website at **www.tarquinbooks.com**
Alternatively, if you would like our latest printed catalogue please contact us by email: info@tarquinbooks.com phone: 0870 143 2568 or write to us at Tarquin Publications, 99 Hatfield Road, St Albans, Herts, AL1 4JL, United Kingdom.